CORVETTE MILESTONES

Mike Mueller

Motorbooks International
Publishers & Wholesalers

First published in 1996 by Motorbooks International Publishers & Wholesalers, 729 Prospect Avenue, PO Box 1, Osceola, WI 54020-0001

Motorbooks International is a certified trademark, registered with the United States Patent Office

The information in this book is true and complete to the best of our knowledge. All recommendations are made without any guarantee on the part of the author or Publisher, who also disclaim any liability incurred in connection with the use of this data or specific details

We recognize that some words, model names and designations, for example, mentioned herein are the property of the trademark holder. We use them for identification purposes only. This is not an official publication

Motorbooks International books are also available at discounts in bulk quantity for industrial or sales-promotional use. For details write to Special Sales Manager at the Publisher's address

Library of Congress Cataloging-in-Publication Data Available

ISBN 0-7603-0095-X

On the front cover: This 1990 legendary "King of the Hill" ZR-1 belongs to Ed and Diann Kuziel of Tampa, Florida. The 1956 SR-2 belongs to Bill and Betty Tower of Plant City, Florida.

On the frontispiece: The most distinctive feature of 1953 through 1955 Corvettes was the beautifully detailed "fence mask" headlight stone guard.

On the title page: The 1968 427 Sting Ray was quickly likened to a Coke bottle, with its bulging front and rear quarters and a slimmed-down midsection. This silver one belongs to Guy Landis of Kutztown, Pennsylvania. The blue 1971 454 Stingray belongs to Tom Biltcliff of Kutztown, Pennsylvania.

On the back cover: The 1963 Grand Sport was a purpose-built race car which followed in the footsteps of Duntov's ill-fated SS of 1957. Only the first five of the 125 planned Grand Sports escaped Chevrolet engineering before racing projects were ordered ceased. This one belongs to Bill Tower of Plant City, Florida.

Printed in Hong Kong

CONTENTS

ACKNOWLEDGMENTS

It was an event some seven years in the making, or four decades depending on your perspective. Many of you out there who've lived with and loved America's sports car from its humble birth in 1953 may have wondered if the long-deserved, long-awaited National Corvette Museum would ever open its doors. Originally discussed in 1987, the idea for a four-walled tribute to one of the greatest cars this county has ever produced went through more than its fair share of ups and downs before becoming reality. But reality it finally was, right there before all our eyes. On September 2, 1994, the ribbon across the doors

of Valhalla in Bowling Green, Kentucky, was finally cut.

Everyone was there—Zora Arkus-Duntov, Dave McLellan, Dave Hill, Jim Perkins, and Larry Shinoda. So were the Beach Boys and about 120,000 others. Nearly all the memorable cars were there as well including Duntov's 1957 SS. Mitchell's Stingray racer Manta Ray, Mako Shark, Purple People Eater, "Big Doggie," and the 1 millionth Corvette. About the only major omissions from the lineup during that first overcrowded weekend were the SR-2 and Grand Sport. But if you wanted to see the greatest collection of Corvettes ever, the National Corvette Museum's grand opening represented a once-in-a-lifetime chance to enjoy as many of them as you could possibly imagine, all together under one very high-pitched roof.

But if you were stuck at home, perhaps you could use a little sampling of what that moment was like. While this humble publication can by no means match the

When the National Corvette Museum finally opened in Bowling Green, Kentucky, on Labor Day weekend in 1994, the legendary piece of Corvette history that greeted visitors at the main lobby was Zora Duntov's ill-fated SS racer of 1957. Shown here in front of the museum, the magnesium-bodied SS was returned later that year to its permanent home at the Indianapolis Motor Speedway Hall of Fame museum.

Everyone was there. Zora Duntov. Dave McLellan. Dave Hill. Jim Perkins. Larry Shinoda. The Beach Boys. And about 120,000 others. Nearly all the memorable cars were there as well—Duntov's 1957 SS, Mitchell's Stingray racer, Manta Ray, Mako Shark, Purple People Eater. . . ■

grandeur of the National Corvette Museum, it can offer as much rolling legend as can fit in 96 pages. Sure, not all the greats are here, but many of them are.

Assembling this four-cornered tribute to one of the greatest cars this county has ever produced involved more than a little bit of help from countless Corvette crazies. As usual, I can't get away without mentioning good friends Greg Pernula and Paul Zazarine of Dobbs Publishing in Lakeland, Florida. Greg is editor of *Corvette Fever* and Paul is a former *CF* editor and now one of Dobbs' editorial directors. Major thanks also goes to another good friend and fiberglass fanatic, Ray Quinlan of Champaign, Illinois. And how can I forget my big-block buddies, Guy Landis and Tom Biltcliff, both of Kutztown, Pennsylvania. Pop another Yuengling for me, will ya?

Former National Corvette Museum director Dan Gale deserves my gratitude as well, as does Jim Kelsey at Bill and Dean Carlson's Klassix Auto Museum in Daytona Beach, Florida. The same goes for Jana

McCoy, of Chevrolet Public Relations in Atlanta. It was Jana who has loaned me three new Corvettes over the last few years, all three making appearances on these pages. Additional support and all-around great company came from Roger and Dave Judski, of Roger's Corvette Center in Maitland, Florida, and Brent Ferguson of the Classic Corvettes of Orlando Club in Florida. Yes, Brent, that is your fuelie engine on page 12.

Also, I must throw in a plug for my younger brothers, Dave, Jim and Ken, and my brother-in-law, Frank Young, all in central Illinois. It has been their company during countless Midwest photo junkets that has helped make my long excursions thoroughly enjoyable—and far less exhausting.

Finally comes mention for all the people who really made this book possible—the various collectors who took the time to allow me to photograph their cars. And while they were at it they also made me feel very much at home. In general order of appearance they are:

1967 L88 and 1969 ZL1 Corvettes, Roger and Dave Judski, Roger's Corvette Center, Maitland, Florida; 1968 427 Sting Ray, Guy Landis, Kutztown, Pennsylvania; 1971 454 Stingray convertible, Tom Biltcliff, Kutztown, Pennsylvania; 1990 ZR-1, Ed and Diann Kuziel, Tampa, Florida; 1953 Corvette, Chip Miller, Carlisle, Pennsylvania; 1955 Corvette, Elmer and Dean Puckett, Elgin, Illinois; 1956 "Betty Skelton racer", 1956 SR-2 and 1963 Grand Sport, Bill and Betty Tower, Plant City, Florida; 1957 "Airbox" Corvette, Milton Robson, Gainesville, Georgia; 1961 "Big Tank" Corvette, Elmer and Sharon Lash, Champaign, Illinois; 1963 Z06 Sting Ray, Bob Lojewski, Cook County, Illinois; 1965 fuel-injected Sting Ray, Gary and Carol Licko, Miami, Florida; 1965 396 Sting Ray, Lukason and Son Collection, Florida; 1967 L71 Sting Ray convertible, Chet and Deb Miltenberger, Winter Park, Florida; 1968 L89 Sting Ray, Elmer and Dean Puckett, Elgin, Illinois; 1972 LT-1 Stingray, Steve and Nora Gussack, Winter Springs, Florida; 1978 Limited Edition Indy Pace Car replica, George and Judi Augustine, New Smyrna Beach, Florida; 1984 serial number 00001 Corvette, Dick Gonyer, Bowling Green, Ohio; 1988 35th anniversary Corvette, Don and Denise Sanzera, Marco Island, Florida; 1991 Callaway Twin Turbo Speedster, Milton Robson, Gainesville, Georgia; 1993 40th anniversary ZR-1 "Black Widow," Jerry Crews, Longwood, Florida.

A hearty thank you to everyone.

INTRODUCTION

FOUR DECADES OF LIFE IN THE FAST LANE

Hard to believe, isn't it? Chevrolet's Corvette, that fantastic plastic flight of fancy, is now in its forties, an age when more than a few of us mere mortals are already rapidly rolling towards the bottom of the hill. Not so for this country's only true sports car. Middle-aged status notwithstanding, Chevy's famed fiberglass two-seater is still out there proving it all night, something this sexy plaything has been doing with exceptional flair longer than any other American performance machine. Class? Convenience? A kick-ass reputation as both a straight-line screamer and curve-hugging road rocket? It's all in there in generous portions no

Isn't it amazing what a difference four decades can make? Forty years of rich Corvette heritage was marked in 1993 by a run of exclusive anniversary models, all painted Ruby Red Metallic. In 1953, Chevrolet's little fiberglass two-seater was a roadster in the true sense of the word—side curtains instead of windows and no outside door handles. Today, the Corvette offers as much comfort and convenience as it does performance.

other sports car can match. At least not for the price.

That's not to say competitors haven't tried over the years. Rivals to the throne have come and gone, some weakly, others with bravado, but all in short-lived fashion. Muntz Jet. Nash-Healey. Kaiser-Darrin. Dual-Ghia. A.C. Cobra. And to a degree, Shelby's Mustang and American Motors' AMX. No, Dodge fans, today's Viper doesn't even come close to earning equal billing. Brutish it is. A proven, complete package it's not. Come back in a year or two (or 10), and then maybe we'll talk.

Let's not forget the foreign challengers. M.G. Austin-Healey. Jaguar's various XKs. Porsche. Aston-Martin. Tough competition all, but none of Europe's best (or Japan's) have ever been able to touch the Corvette in the category near and dear to the hearts of most Yankee buyers—value. Look up the dictionary listing for "most bang for the buck" (in world-class sports car terms) and you'll likely see a picture of a Corvette. If

Fuel injection appeared as a Corvette option, at a cost of $484.20, for the first time in 1957. Various modifications raised "fuelie" output over the years before the Rochester injection equipment was deleted after 1965.

you take $40,000 out today and come home with as much relatively roomy (again, in sports car terms) comfort, prestigious pizzazz and pulsating performance as offered by Chevy's all-American two-seater, you've undoubtedly had to settle for something less than new. Or far less exciting.

And to think General Motors' decision-makers almost gave up on Chevrolet's fiberglass fantasy for lack of interest after about two years on the road.

When the first Corvette rolled off its makeshift assembly line in Flint, Michigan, on June 30, 1953, it certainly fit the classic sports car mold, what with its somewhat crude folding top and plastic side curtains in place of

roll-up windows. All 300 first-edition roadsters were painted Polo White with red interiors. And all were powered by a muscled-up version of Chevrolet's yeoman "Stovebolt" six-cylinder backed by a less-than-desirable two-speed Powerglide automatic.

Obviously, "limited" was a fair description in more ways than one. And adding exterior paint choices in 1954 did little to change that fact. With nearly a third of the 3,640 1954 Corvettes built sitting unsold at year's end, many at Chevrolet were wondering if it wasn't just best to cut and run.

But they didn't, and the Corvette quickly found its niche after V-8 power and a manual transmission were added to the mix in

That large, gold "V" tacked over the Chevrolet emblem on this 1955 Corvette signifies the presence of a 265ci V-8, the engine that basically saved America's only sports car from quick extinction.

It certainly fit the classic sports car mold. ∎

1955. Nearly four decades later, Chevrolet rolled out its 1 millionth Corvette—appropriately enough, an Arctic White convertible with red interior—on July 2, 1992, proving that someone at GM knew what they were doing. Among others, names like Harley Earl, Ed Cole, Zora Arkus-Duntov, Bill Mitchell, and two Daves, McLellan and Hill, quickly come to mind.

It was long-time GM styling mogul Earl who first campaigned for the little two-seat sportster in the early 1950s. Cole supplied all-important support for the project early on, first as Chevrolet's chief engineer, then as the division's general manager beginning in July 1956. And Duntov, the so-called "father of the Corvette," needs no introduction. After Zora retired as Corvette chief engineer in 1975, Dave McClellan took his place, followed by Dave Hill in 1992. As for Mitchell,

he replaced Earl as head GM stylist in 1958, then was responsible for the startling Sting Ray transformation unveiled for 1963. Of course, the list of other prime movers and major players both inside GM and out runs much longer than this. But they must remain in the shadows for now to allow the cars themselves to shine in the spotlight supplied by this ninety-six-page mini-epic.

A similar challenge appeared when faced with trying to properly honor the major milestones in the Corvette's rich forty-odd-year history. Although beginning the story is easy enough, where do you end? Perhaps discounting, with all gentleness, the comparatively weak-kneed models built in the performance-starved late 1970s and early 1980s, hasn't damn near every Corvette built been a truly great American car? And in the years since—especially after Chevrolet introduced the wonderfully efficient, exceptionally potent second-generation LT1 small-block V-8 in 1992—hasn't each succeeding model briefly represented the best Corvette yet?

As fuel injection was falling by the wayside in 1965, the Corvette was receiving its first big-block V-8, the 396ci Mk IV. Chevy's "Mk motors" had debuted in 427ci racing form at the Daytona 500 in 1963. As a Corvette option, the 396 Mk IV rated at a healthy 425hp, enough muscle to make the Sting Ray America's most powerful production car this side of Shelby's 427 Cobra Euro-Yankee hybrid.

LEFT
"If you take that off," claimed GM styling chief Bill Mitchell, "you might as well forget the whole thing." Mitchell was referring to his pet Sting Ray styling element, the so-called "stinger" that separated the all-new 1963 Corvette's rear windows. Among others, Zora Duntov didn't like the split-window theme due to the way it hindered rearward vision. Despite Mitchell's emotional appeal, Chevrolet did "take that off" for 1964. And didn't forget the whole thing.

Nonetheless, many great moments do stand out more than others. And although determining which of these ranks among the greatest may represent a tough task, following the everyday Corvette legacy through its various ups and downs and ins and outs, isn't all that difficult.

The Corvette was built in St. Louis, Missouri, from December 1953 through July 1981, and in Bowling Green, Kentucky, from June 1981 to present. It has evolved through four definable "generations," beginning with the solid-axle variants of 1953 through 1962. The so-called "mid-year" models of 1963-67 make up the second generation, followed by the third running from 1968 to 1982. After the "hiccup" year of 1983, an all-new Cor-vette appeared for 1984 to kick off the fourth generation, which is coming to an end as we speak. Chevrolet's "C-5"—"5" for fifth generation—awaits its debut, either as a 1997 or 1998 model, depending on how soon Dave Hill's men decide to stop teasing us.

A new Corvette body for 1968 (right) drew both raves and complaints for its sexy shape, some saying it was "painfully too American." Truly American in this case are the two big-block V-8s beneath these Corvettes' hoods. The silver 1968 has the 427 derivative of Chevy's Mk IV big-block; the blue 1971 convertible has the larger 454, introduced for 1970. Big-block Corvette production lasted until 1974, when the last 454 Sting Ray was built.

All Corvettes were convertibles through 1962, with an optional removable hardtop available after 1956. Roll-up windows were added that year as well, making Chevrolet's sports car more socially acceptable from a

LEFT
A potent pair indeed. Both the aluminum-head L88 (back) and all-aluminum ZL1 427s were jokingly rated at only 430hp. Actual output zoomed past 500 for these race-ready rockets. Only twenty 1967 L88 coupes were built, while two 1969 ZL1s escaped Chevrolet Engineering.

Yankee perspective. Independent rear suspension and a coupe model first appeared in 1963, when all Corvettes also became Sting Rays—a name that stuck until it fell by the wayside after 1976. From 1969 to 1976, "Stingray" was used. Beginning in 1976, all Corvettes were coupes as the droptop model was deleted, only to reappear in 1986. Single headlamps were used from 1953 through 1957, followed by dual units in 1958. Hideaway headlights have been the norm since the Sting Ray's appearance in 1963.

Easily recognized by its widened tail section, added to help house some serious rubber in back, Chevrolet's first ZR-1 Corvette emerged in 1990 to do battle with the world's best sports car. With a top end of nearly 180mph, the 375hp LT5-powered ZR-1 was an able competitor. LT5 output jumped to 405hp in 1993. ZR-1 production ended two years later.

As for power, Chevrolet's ground-breaking 265ci overhead-valve V-8 replaced the valiant, yet disappointing six in 1955. Optional dual four-barrel carbs appeared the following year. Then came fuel injection in 1957, the same year the enlarged 283 small-block V-8 and available four-speed manual transmission debuted. Standard displacement grew to 327ci in 1962, when only a single four-barrel was offered atop the three available carbureted V-8s. The last "fuelie" Sting Ray was built in 1965 as the Corvette's first big-block V-8 was appearing as the top power option. Originally offered in 396ci form, the legendary Mk IV big-block bully was bumped up to 427ci in 1966, then to a whopping 454ci in 1970.

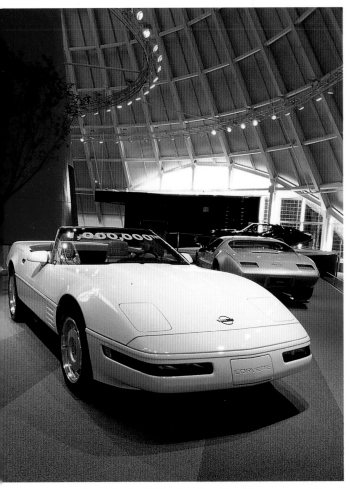

On July 2, 1992, the Bowling Green assembly plant in Kentucky rolled out the celebrated 1 millionth Corvette, a white convertible with red interior. Chevrolet later donated that car to Bowling Green's National Corvette Museum, where it resides today.

Independent rear suspension and a coupe model first appeared in 1963, when all Corvettes also became Sting Rays, a name that stuck until it fell by the wayside after 1976. ∎

Meanwhile, small-block performance was progressing at full speed as the 370hp LT-1 350 was introduced for the 1970 Corvette. The most powerful carbureted small-block (the fuel-injected 327 rated at 375 horses in top tune and the ZR-1's injected LT5 later hit 405hp) ever offered under that long fiberglass hood was the

first-generation LT-1. It lasted but three years before falling victim to rising insurance costs, ever-tightening emissions standards and tougher federal safety specifications. The dreaded fuel crunch of the 1970s also helped bring down the 454 Stingray, with the last big-block Corvette rolling out of St. Louis in 1974.

Carburetors disappeared after 1981 as "Cross Fire" injection was made standard for the 1982 Corvette, a car which, like its early forerunners, came only with an automatic transmission. After a one-year drought, a four-speed manual returned to its proper place on the options list when the redesigned fourth-generation Corvette appeared as a 1984 model. A true "fuelie" Corvette returned in 1985 with the arrival of Bosch's tuned-port injection setup, which carried over atop the sensational 300hp, 5.7-liter, second-generation LT1 V-8, introduced in 1992. The TPI LT1 remained the Corvette's heart and soul until replaced by the sequential-port fuel-injected LT1 in 1994.

Improvements in 1994 made the LT1 feel even stronger even though advertised output remained at 300 horses. Modifications included trading the previously used multi-port fuel injection for a sequential-port setup. Speed-density fuel calibration was also superseded by a more precise mass-air flow calibration system.

RIGHT
Beneath the 1993 40th anniversary Corvette's Ruby Red Metallic skin beat the heart of the exceptional 5.7-liter LT1 small-block V-8, a 300hp thriller first introduced in 1992. By 1994, the LT1 had become the backbone of Chevrolet's performance lineup, powering everything from Z28 Camaro to Impala SS.

*H*asn't damn near every Corvette built
been a truly great American car? ■

Honors in recent decades include three trips around the legendary Brickyard in Indianapolis as the prestigious pace car for the Indy 500. In all three years, 1978, 1986, and 1995, street-going replicas of those official Indy pacers were sold to the public. Special high-profile models were also created to mark the Corvette's 25th, 35th and 40th birthdays in 1978, 1988 and 1993, respectively. And equally special "Collector Editions" were offered in 1982 and presently for 1996. New also for 1996 is the Corvette Grand Sport, a modern-day, regular-production commemoration of its all-out race-ready namesake of 1963. Power for the new Grand Sport comes from a 330hp LT4 V-8.

But easily the greatest moment in Corvette history came some six years ago when the feared and revered ZR-1 debuted as a 1990 model. The ZR-1's high-tech aluminum LT5 V-8, a 375hp 5.7-liter small-block with dual overhead cams and 11:1 compression, quickly helped remind many by-standers of some earlier exotic Corvettes. Prime examples include the 425hp

LS-6 of 1971, the all-aluminum ZL-1 of 1969 and the aluminum-head L88s built from 1967 to 1969. But unlike those grumpy, race-bred, ultra-low-production beasts, the ZR-1 was an animal that was easy enough to get along with on the street, yet more than capable of ripping the lungs out of any and all stoplight challengers. And it also stuck around long enough to make a noticeable impression, although market pressures finally helped bring about the ZR-1's demise in 1995.

Even without the ZR-1 to lead the way, Chevrolet's Corvette remains in 1996 every bit as great as so many of its legendary ancestors. Four decades down the road, and America's only sports car is still rockin' as strong as ever. How many of us today wish we could say that?

RIGHT
Forty-three years after its birth, America's only sports car is still running strong for 1996. Big news this year involves the debut of Chevrolet's optional 330hp LT4. Standard power still comes from the tried-and-true 300hp LT1.

HUMBLE BEGINNINGS

Okay, so it wasn't all that hot of a car, what with its somewhat ho-hum six-cylinder powerplant, decidedly non-sporty two-speed Powerglide automatic transmission and yeoman chassis. But if you want to talk about the greatest of the great from the Corvette bloodline, you have to kick off the discussion somewhere.

Seriously, though, Chevrolet's first Corvette certainly deserves more than a backhanded compliment or two. Its ground-breaking status as this country's first true "mainstream" sports car built by a major manufacturer is enough to forever honor those 300 Polo White 1953 roadsters as milestones in American automotive history.

All 300 1953 Corvettes were painted Polo White with red interiors. And like so many of its sports car rivals from Europe, Chevy's fiberglass two-seat roadster didn't have exterior door handles or roll-up windows. Aftermarket companies would soon be offering an available bolt-on hardtop, something Chevrolet would make official in 1956, the same year roll-up windows and external door handles were added to the mix.

That the major manufacturer was Chevrolet—a leader in frugal practicality—only served to help make the Corvette's birth even more historic. After 1953, more and more buyers changed the way they looked at that signature Bow-Tie. This was due to the debut of Chevy's little two-seat sportster, followed two years later by the arrival of the division's first modern overhead-valve V-8. And from there, the low-priced market would never be the same.

Before 1953, the low-priced field was the last place a speed-conscious customer looked for performance, let alone sports car performance. Yet at the time, sports cars were reasonably popular in America, most of them being imported from Europe. All previous attempts to market Yankee reactions to this European postwar invasion had basically consisted of low-production independent efforts or special hybrids made up of American engines in foreign bodies. Chevy's entry into this field, however, was red, white and blue through and through.

Much work went into designing the first Corvette's dual exhaust outlets to prevent staining the bodywork in back. The car's folding top didn't do much for those low lines, credited originally to long-time GM styling head Harley Earl.

Although much of the credit for developing the Corvette falls on the shoulders of long-time chief engineer Zora Duntov, he wasn't working for General Motors when the project began. By the time he joined Chevrolet's research and development team in May 1953, the wheels were already turning and initial production start-up was one month away. While Duntov would soon boldly make his presence known, it was actually Harley Earl, legendary GM styling head from 1927 to 1958, who may well represent the true "father of the Corvette."

Earl began toying with the idea of a regular-production sporty two-seater in the fall of 1951, after creating a pair of high-profile two-place Buick showcars. A plaster model was ready by April 1952, and support for the project came the following month from Chevrolet chief engineer Ed Cole. Chevy engineers were brought into the fray in June, kicking off a mad rush to build a showcar prototype for GM's upcoming Motorama at New York's Waldorf-Astoria hotel in January 1953.

Under Earl's direction, designer Robert McLean laid out the basic platform on a 102-inch wheelbase. The chassis was a mixture of stock Chevy parts (front suspension), specially adapted off-the-shelf components (steering and rear axle) and newly designed pieces (the rigid X-member frame). On top went a definitely unique fiberglass shell, supplied once regular production began by

Along with painful fact that all 1953-54 Corvettes used Chevrolet's mundane two-speed Powerglide automatic transmission, customers also found fault with the location of the tachometer, hidden here behind the steering wheel in the center of the dash. Most agreed the passenger had a better view of rpm readout than the driver.

Its ground-breaking status as this country's first true "mainstream" sports car built by a major manufacturer represents grounds enough to forever honor those 300 Polo White 1953 roadsters as milestones in American automotive history. ■

the Molded Fiber Glass Body Company of Ashtabula, Ohio. Although quickly dated as the style-conscious 1950s marched on, the original Corvette image was well-received in 1953, since it was considered both modern and sporty.

For power, Cole's engineers tweaked Chevy's tried-and-true 235ci six-cylinder up to 150hp from the maximum 115 horses

produced in passenger car applications. A boost in compression from 7.5:1 to 8:1, a bumpier mechanical cam, dual exhausts, and three Carter carburetors on a special side-draft aluminum manifold did the trick. As mentioned, Cole's men then backed up the "Blue Flame Six" with a floor-shifted Powerglide automatic, a move that became the largest target for slings and arrows once the exciting Corvette hit the road in the summer of 1953.

Chevrolet took a defensive stand right away concerning the Corvette's automatic-only status. According to research and development head Maurice Olley, "the use of an automatic transmission has been criticized by those who believe sports car enthusiasts want nothing but a four-speed crash shift. The answer is that the typical sports car enthusiast, like the 'average man,' is an imaginary quantity. Also, as the sports car appeals to a wider and wider section of the public, the center of gravity of this theoretical individual is shifting from the austerity of the pioneer towards the lux-

Additional exterior colors were added to the Corvette appeal in 1955, the same year Chevrolet's first overhead-valve V-8 appeared. While the six-cylinder remained available, up five horses that year, the majority of 1955 Corvettes featured the 265ci V-8. And some cars late in the year were equipped with the newly offered three-speed manual transmission.

Chrome dress-up only helped sweeten the pot for V-8 Corvette buyers in 1955. With a four-barrel "Power Pak," the 265 V-8 was rated at 195hp beneath a fiberglasss hood.

Three sidedraft carburetors and a split exhaust manifold represented the most obvious modifications that helped transform Chevy's durable "Stovebolt" six into the 1953 Corvette's Blue Flame six. Output was 150hp for the 235ci in-line powerplant.

ury of modern ideas." Concluded Olley, "there is no need to apologize for the performance of this car with its automatic transmission."

Others weren't so sure. "That statement should get a rise from 100,000 *Road & Track* readers," wrote *R&T's* John Bond, who nonetheless generally praised the 1953 Corvette for its performance from a ride and handling perspective. The automotive press, however, pointed out that the Corvette would never be able to compete with foreign rivals on a track thanks to that damned Powerglide. On the street, however, it was another story. According to *Road & Track's* test, an early six-cylin-der Corvette could do 0-60mph in 11 seconds and the quarter-mile in 17.9 seconds—not bad at all for the time. Top end listed at 107mph.

Generally speaking, it was a decent start for a new car hastily created, basically from scratch, to compete in a completely unfamiliar field. Nonetheless, American buyers were not entirely impressed and Corvette sales lagged well below projections through 1954, causing GM officials to consider killing the project. Decision time came in 1955, a year when only 700 Corvettes were built. Hope for the future, however, had already arrived in the form of the Corvette's first V-8.

After nearly a third of the 3,640 Corvettes built for 1954 remained unsold at year's end, Chevrolet officials pulled in the reins, building only 700 more for 1955.

Work had begun on a V-8 Corvette—using Chevrolet's prototype for its all-new OHV V-8 scheduled for passenger car debut in 1955—in the spring of 1954, under the direction of performance development head Mauri Rose. While adding V-8 power to the package was undoubtedly the right thing to do to keep the project alive, the appearance in February 1954 of a plastic mockup from Ford featuring a concept soon to be called "personal luxury," also helped. That mockup was for the legendary Thunderbird which debuted in October 1954 with, among other attractions, a standard V-8 beneath the long, scooped hood. Although the two-seat T-bird wasn't exactly direct competition, it was more than enough of a threat to inspire rapid-fire reaction in the Chevrolet camp.

So, an optional V-8 joined the standard 155hp six in the Corvette lineup for 1955. At 265ci, Chevrolet's new OHV V-8 was rated at 195hp beneath a fiberglass hood, thanks to the addition of a four-barrel "Power Pak" and special cam. Corvettes equipped with the 265ci V-8—the vast majority in 1955 were—were identified by the large "V" emblem added to the "Chevrolet" fender script. A long-awaited, three-speed manual transmission was promised for 1955, but it didn't arrive until well into the model year. Estimates put manual transmission 1955 Corvette production at perhaps 70 or 80.

Predictably, performance improved considerably with two more cylinders to help pull the load. According to a *Road & Track* test, rest to 60mph required only 8.7 seconds for the 1955 V-8 Corvette, which topped out at 119mph. A quarter-mile went by in a relatively scant 16.5 seconds. Although most critics still complained about the brakes and ever-present Powerglide, it was clear the Corvette was on the right track to recovery, thanks to the welcomed power boost.

All other complaints would be addressed soon enough; in 1955, simply saving the car from extinction was the sole goal. And the first V-8 Corvette helped do just that.

RACING IMPROVES THE BREED

Chevrolet officials from the beginning chose to throw in a disclaimer when referring to their first-edition Corvette in print, stating that Chevy's polite two-seater was not intended for use as a "racing sports car." As it was, they really didn't need to point out what quickly became obvious to both buyers and innocent bystanders alike. Critics in the press were more than willing to explain how the wimpy Powerglide automatic would never succeed on a track. And even though it was by no means a weakling, the early Corvette's Blue Flame Six certainly had room for improvement.

A few chassis tweaks, an all-new OHV V-8 mated to a manual transmission, and the

Featuring unique aluminum trim throughout to help save weight, this Smokey Yunick-prepped 1956 Corvette was one of the three cars taken to Daytona in February 1956 for NASCAR's annual Speed Week trials. Originally driven on the sands by Betty Skelton, the car today resides in Bill Tower's noted Corvette collection. Tower also owns an SR-2 and 1963 Grand Sport.

emergence of chief Corvette engineer Zora Arkus-Duntov, and America's only sports car was almost totally transformed. Following the 265ci V-8's debut in 1955, an exciting new body appeared for 1956. Appeasements to Yankee sensibilities produced roll-up windows, external door handles and an optional removable hardtop.

More importantly, at least from a horsepower hound's perspective, the 265ci V-8 was boosted to 225hp with the addition of RPO (regular production option) 469, made up of two Carter four-barrel carburetors. And if you really wanted to get serious, you could order the so-called "Duntov cam," a high-lift bumpstick specified "for racing purposes only." Clearly, Chevrolet's attitude about the Corvette had changed. Listed under RPO 449 or 448, depending on your source, the Duntov cam was only available with RPO 469. No official advertised horsepower figure was given, although most sources put output for the special-cam engine at 240hp.

Various modification tricks used on the "Betty Skelton racer" included these brake-cooling ducts. Feeding outside air through vented backing plates into the drums, this setup would soon become a regular Corvette option. These ducts would later come to be called "elephant ears."

RIGHT
Bill Tower's 1956 SR-2 was the second of three built. After Harley Earl ordered the first SR-2 for his son Jerry, Bill Mitchell requested one be built for himself. SR-2 number two's competition debut came in 1957 at Daytona, where Buck Baker recorded a flying-mile time of 152mph.

Along with the optional removable hardtop, this 1957 fuel-injected Corvette also features wider 15x5.5 wheels, as identified by the small hub caps. This fuelie is an "Airbox" car as well, meaning it is equipped with special duct-work included to help supply cooler, denser outside air direct access to the Rochester injection setup. Only 43 Air-box Corvettes were built for 1957.

Now armed with a race-ready rocket, Duntov set out to prove that his baby was no longer intended solely for streetside duty. In February 1956, he took a three-car team to Daytona Beach, Florida, for NASCAR's annual Speed Week trials. Join-ing him were veteran race driver John Fitch and champion aerobatic pilot Betty Skelton. By the time the three finally slowed down, Duntov had established a new sports car flying-mile standard of 150.533mph, while Fitch had set a two-way record at 145.543mph. Skelton man-aged a 137.773mph two-way clocking.

Corvettes quickly established themselves as able-bodied competitors in Sports Car Club of America (SCCA) stock-class racing. ∎

Lightened throughout, the SR-2 also featured many modifications that may or may not have been retrofitted, including a four-speed manual transmission, equipment that didn't become a Corvette option until 1957. Notice the twin racing windscreens and the cooling louvers added to the hood.

Fitch then led a four-car effort south to Sebring for the 12-Hour endurance event in March with less impressive results. Even Duntov knew the Corvette still wasn't ready to take on Europe's best in endurance competition. Going flat-out in speed trials was one thing; slowing and speeding up around twists and turns was an entirely different ball game which Europeans knew how to play all too well. From the beginning, Duntov recognized he would need much more of a sports car to beat foreign rivals on their turf.

Nonetheless, Corvettes quickly established themselves as able-bodied competitors in Sports Car Club of America (SCCA) stock-class racing. Armed with an ever-growing arsenal of hot factory parts such as special brakes and beefed suspension, Dr. Dick Thompson first proved that Chevy's fiberglass two-seater could indeed be used as a racing sports car. In 1956 he claimed his first SCCA production-class championship at the wheel of a Corvette. Thompson won again in 1957, 1962 and 1963, and added an SCCA C-Modified title in 1960.

The Airbox arrangement's cool-air plenum can be seen at the top of this photo directly inside the fender—it's connected by that flexible duct to the Rochester unit. Listed under RPO 579E, the Airbox 283 V-8 rated the same as the top 1957 fuelie small-block, 283hp.

Underhood crowding created by the Airbox ductwork meant the tachometer drive had to be relocated, which in turn meant the tach itself had to be moved from its typical spot in the dash to atop the steering column. The column-mounted tach is one of the easiest clues to the identity of an Airbox Corvette. Notice the medallion located in the opening left behind by the remounted tach.

*D*untov's SS, designated XP-64, was hastily created beginning in July 1956 for competition at Sebring in March 1957. ∎

A heavy-duty racing-type suspension and specially cooled racing brakes officially appeared as a regular-production Corvette option in 1957, as did a welcomed four-speed manual transmission. Appearing for the first time was a Positraction rear axle and wider wheels. Reportedly, some racers were also supplied with a few oversized fuel tanks, a feature that would eventually end up on the options list in 1959. But the biggest news was the arrival of Ramjet fuel injection.

LEFT
Truly innovative throughout, the magnesium bodied SS racer of 1957 nonetheless fell victim to hasty development. Even though it possessed the power to compete with Europe's best, the car carried too many gremlins with it onto the track at Sebring in March 1957. It retired after only 23 laps.

Once atop the 1957 Corvette's enlarged 283ci small-block, Ramjet fuel injection, supplied by Rochester, boosted output to 283 horses in top form. It was the second time a Detroit V-8 reached the one-horsepower-per-cubic-inch milestone—Chrysler had offered an optional 355hp 354 Hemi V-8 for its 300B luxury cruiser the year before. Although a bit finicky, the fuelie 283ci was capable of powering a 1957 Corvette from zero to 60mph in less than six seconds. Simply sizzling.

A Chevrolet team returned to Sebring in 1957, but early Corvette competition efforts weren't limited to production-class racing. The distinctive SR-2 "prototype racers" had emerged the year before. Conceived by Harley Earl for his son Jerry, the first Corvette SR-2 featured a custom fiberglass shell on a race-ready chassis. The SR-2 incorporated all the heavy-duty suspension and brake tricks Fitch had put to the test at Sebring in 1956. In Chevrolet engineering lingo, those beefed parts were known as "SR" components, which may or may not have stood for "Sports Racing" or "Sebring Racer." Either

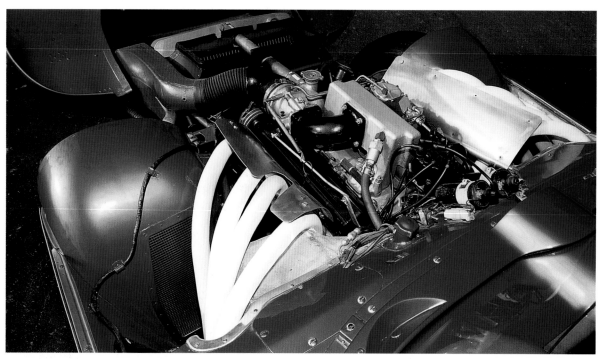

Powering the SS was a modified fuel-injected small-block with aluminum heads and a magnesium oil pan. Additional tweaks included revised valves and a special injection manifold. Dyno tests in 1957 put output at 307hp.

Veteran driver John Fitch and co-driver Piero Taruffi sat here on race day at Sebring in 1957 after Stirling Moss and Juan Fangio both withdrew from the SS team just prior to the event. One of the SS racer's many glitches involved heat buildup inside the cockpit. Both Fitch and Taruffi were literally boiled as the magnesium shell didn't dissipate heat like its fiberglass counterpart.

"Sports Racing" or "Sebring Racer." Either way, Fitch's Corvette factory racers were the first "SRs," meaning any variation to follow was naturally the second. Thus the "SR-2."

Jerry Earl's SR-2—shop order number 90090—was built in about four weeks, leading some to believe its modified body was simply dropped right onto an existing Sebring chassis. Supposedly, an off-the-lot 1956 Corvette went into Engineering in May and came out as the SR-2 in June. Presto.

On top of that race-ready chassis was a metallic blue body wearing an extended snout and bright aluminum bodyside cove panels. Louvers on the hood and vents in each door were functional; the former cool-

O nce atop the 1957 Corvette's enlarged 283ci small-block, Ramjet fuel injection, supplied by Rochester, boosted output to 283 horses in top form. It was the second time a Detroit V8 reached the one-horsepower-per-cubic-inch milestone. ∎

ing the engine, the latter cooling the rear brakes. Twin short windscreens were used up front, while a small tailfin was added down the center of the decklid in back.

Racing modifications included cutout exhausts, an oversized fuel tank and Halibrand knock-off mag wheels. Interior treatment, however, was not at all like a race car's. Looking more like a showcar, Earl's SR-2 featured blue vinyl seats, custom instrumentation in a stainless-steel dash panel, and a wood-rimmed steering wheel. But all the extra flash translated into extra weight, which resulted in a disappointing competition debut at Wisconsin's Elkhart Lake in June 1956.

Earl's SR-2 was then lightened, but real success didn't come until the car was sold in 1957 to Jim Jeffords, driver for Chicago dealer Nickey Chevrolet. By that time, the first SR-2 featured a larger, reshaped tailfin offset to the driver's side to serve as a headrest and rollbar. The new design was added at Earl's request, after he saw it on the second SR-2 built for Bill Mitchell. As for SR-2

number one, in Jeffords' able hands it raced to a SCCA B/Production championship in 1958.

Mitchell's red-and-white SR-2 debuted in February 1957 during Daytona's Speed Week trials. There, Buck Baker recorded a flying-mile speed of 152.886 mph in the "high-finned" car, which finished sixteenth at Sebring a month later.

A third "low-finned" SR-2 was built for GM president Harlow Curtice. Basically a stock 1956 Corvette underneath, Curtice's SR-2 was meant only for the show circuit. Metallic blue paint was again used, as were Dayton wire wheels and a removable stainless steel hardtop.

All three SR-2s still survive, after passing through various owners' hands and experiencing a modification or two along the way. Originally powered by dual-carb small-blocks, the trio are now fuel injected. Four-speed transmissions are also on board even though, like Rochester fuel injection, a four-speed didn't appear as a Corvette option until 1957. Some bystanders believe

This is one of Larry Shinoda's drawings for the CERV 1 test vehicle. Built in 1960, CERV 1, among other things, established many of the design parameters for the 1963 Sting Ray's independent rear suspension.

RIGHT
Penned by stylist Larry Shinoda, the XP-755 Mako Shark was built in 1961 as a personal car for Shinoda's boss, Bill Mitchell. XP-755 borrowed many of its lines from the XP-720 project, which was the prototype for the all-new 1963 Sting Ray. When another Mako Shark styling exercise appeared in 1965, Mitchell's car became known as the Mako Shark I. Today, the Mako Shark I resides at the National Corvette Museum in Bowling Green, Kentucky.

the prototype installation tale, while others simply believe the fuelie/four-speed equipment came via a retrofit.

While SR-2 racers represented independent efforts, the next great Corvette competition project was a factory job from top to bottom. As previously mentioned, Duntov always wanted a world-class racing machine. And his first attempt to transform his ideal into reality came in the form of the SS racer of 1957.

Duntov's SS, designated XP-64, was hastily created beginning in July 1956 for competition at Sebring in March 1957. It

Adding the oversized 24-gallon fuel tank meant the removable hardtop option was also required since the tank took up the space behind the seat where the folding top normally resided. The oversized tank was first officially offered for 1959, although some reportedly had been supplied to racers as early as 1957.

was an all-out, purpose-built machine, with its low-slung tubular space frame and lightweight magnesium body. Aluminum was used throughout, including the gearbox, radiator and cylinder heads on the modified 283 fuelie V-8. Coilover shocks were at all four corners, an independent de Dion rearend was in back, and the brakes were finned drums with the rear pair mounted inboard on the differential to reduce unsprung weight. An innovative, servo-controlled booster system was also incorporated to help prevent rear wheel brake lockup. Along with the one beautiful blue SS built in Chevy Engineering, Duntov's crew also fashioned a crude fiberglass-bodied test mule counterpart.

LEFT
This 1961 fuelie features various racing-inspired options, including wide wheels, quicker steering and heavy-duty suspension with specially cooled brakes. But rarest of the bunch is LPO (limited-production option) 1625, the so-called "big tank." Notice the exposed fuel filler cap behind the door—it represented one of the modifications made to mount the larger tank behind this 1961 Corvette's seat.

On paper, the SS project certainly looked promising. And early tests of the white SS mule at Sebring were impressive. But too much work was rushed trying to make the tight Sebring deadline. Problems appeared almost immediately on race day for the blue SS, including rising cockpit temperatures, fading brakes and a loose rear suspension. Only twenty-three laps were completed before the SS was forced to retire from the 12-Hour endurance event.

Chevy's vaunted small-block displaced 265 cubes when introduced in 1955, then grew to 283ci in 1957. In 1962, the last year for the solid-axle first-generation Corvette, the small-block again grew, this time to 327ci. This is the top carbureted 327 for 1962. Output was 340 horses, compared to 360 for its fuel-injected counterpart. Only single four-barrel carburetors were offered in 1962; dual carbs were last offered in 1961.

A few chasis tweaks, an all-new OHV V8 mated to a manual trans, and the emergence of chief Corvette engineer Zora Arkus-Duntov later and America's only sports car was nearly totally transformed. ∎

Then, any hopes of going back to the drawing board and trying again at Le Mans later that summer were dashed, once the Automobile Manufacturers Association (AMA) issued its so-called ban on factory racing involvement. One can only wonder what might have been, especially after Duntov's SS hit 183mph at GM's Phoenix proving grounds in December 1958.

The lone blue SS made one more cameo appearance in February 1959, turning a 155-mph lap around NASCAR's brand-new Daytona International Speedway during opening ceremonies. Later, the car was donated to the Indianapolis Motor Speedway Hall of Fame Museum where it still resides today.

As for the fiberglass SS mule, it also survives, although not in its original form. During the winter of 1958-59, it was acquired by GM styling head Bill Mitchell. Its chassis was used as a base for his XP-87 Stingray racer, a car that provided more than one styling trick later used on the regular-production Sting Ray in 1963. With Dr.

Dick Thompson at the wheel, Mitchell's Stingray roared to an SCCA C/Modified championship in 1960.

With the AMA "ban" in place by the summer of 1957, Chevrolet was forced to cut back on its factory racing efforts. While factory support of certain Corvette racers—namely Dr. Thompson—continued, it was primarily the covert, "back-door" type. Clearly obvious, however, was the long list of factory options still present and accounted for after 1957: big metallic brakes with special cooling ducts, quicker steering gear, bigger wheels, and beefed suspension components. Duntov even tested a set of weight-saving aluminum fuelie cylinder heads in 1960, although that option was quickly discontinued when production defects couldn't be cured. All this purposeful equipment and more was on the option list, as were loads of fuel-injected power—up to 360 horses worth by 1962.

And American sports car devotees who thought it just couldn't get any better needed only to wait another year.

ENTER THE STING RAY

It may easily rank among the most startling transformations in American automotive history. When Zora Duntov, Bill Mitchell and crew took what was already one of this country's most startling automobiles and redesigned it for 1963, they succeeded in creating a true modern classic. It is this car that most often comes to mind when even the most casual observer thinks "Corvette."

From nose to tail, the all-new 1963 Sting Ray was a stunner. "This is the one we've been waiting for," wrote *Motor Trend's* Roger Huntington. "This is a modern sports car." Even Duntov himself was finally satisfied: "For the first time I now have a Corvette I can be proud to drive in Europe."

Zora Duntov tried again to build a world-class racing Corvette late in 1962. But plans to build 125 lightweight Grand Sports failed when GM's anti-performance overlords shot things down. Only five Grand Sports were built before the ax fell early in 1963. Two of these were later converted into roadsters.

Lower, thinner, shorter and riding on a compact 98-inch wheelbase (down from the previous 102-inch chassis), the sleek, sexy Sting Ray was nonetheless more comfortable inside than its solid-axle forerunner, thanks to repositioned seating in a redesigned frame. And innovative (at least in Yankee terms), independent rear suspension improved both ride and handling.

On top of it all was Mitchell's alarming new Corvette shell—available for the first time in coupe form—with hideaway headlights in front, and crisp, curvaceous lines throughout. It featured a tapered roofline with Mitchell's pet split-window "stinger" theme in back. Any way you looked at it, the car was a killer, although many critics—including Duntov—didn't think much of the split rear windows. So, despite Mitchell's adamant defenses, the stinger was deleted in 1964.

Initial demand for the attractive Sting Ray was so great, that adding an extra shift at the St. Louis plant couldn't even help keep up. Overall, 1963 sales (coupes and convert-

Beefy brakes were part of the Z06 deal. Included was a dual-circuit power booster; enlarged, finned drums; sintered cerametallix linings; and special cooling gear. Rubberized "elephant ear" ducts directed airflow through vented backing plates where an internal fan helped stir things around. The drums themselves were also vented. One drawback to these brutish binders was that they barely worked at all before they were warmed up.

TOP RIGHT
Grand Sport racers were amazingly stock looking inside, although a closer inspection would reveal the presence of a 200mph speedometer. Also barely noticeable just above the passenger seat is a movie camera used by Chevrolet engineers to document on-track testing action.

BOTTOM RIGHT
Beneath all that plumbing is a 377ci aluminum small-block. Those are four 58mm Weber side-draft two-barrels on a cross-ram intake. The Webers on the left feed the cylinder bank on the right and vice versa. Original plans to equip the Grand Sport with the 377 small-block were canceled when the project itself was shut down by GM's front office in January 1963. Grand Sports were first powered by less exotic fuel-injected 327s. Various other power sources followed over the years.

Sting Rays were delivered directly into the hands of prominent racers in October 1962. The competition debut for this race-ready Corvette came October 13 in Riverside, California, at the same event that showcased the first of Carroll Shelby's little Ford-powered Cobras. Having had their way in SCCA competition throughout the late 1950s and early 1960s, competition Corvettes were soon left in the dust by Shelby's Cobras. But how could Chevy engineers have foreseen this occurrence in 1962, especially considering the tools they were about to use?

RPO Z06 consisted of every hot part on the Corvette shelf. Mandatory features included the L84 fuelie 327, backed by its close-ratio Muncie four-speed and Positraction rearend. Initially listed were heavy-duty suspension parts, special "cerametallix" power brakes with unique cooling features, an oversized 36.5-gallon fiberglass fuel tank, and five cast-aluminum knock-off wheels. In December, Chevrolet temporarily canceled the knock-off option, due to production difficulties, and removed the big

ibles) soared by 50 percent to a new high of 21,513 cars. Still a polite tourer in base form with a 250hp 327, backed by a three-speed manual, the 1963 Sting Ray could typically be transformed into a street killer, thanks to a long list of options. Most prominent, from a power perspective, was the 360hp fuel-injected small-block, RPO L84.

Last, but certainly not least on that list was RPO Z06, the Special Performance Equipment group. Any questions about the intentions of this potent package were quickly answered once the first six Z06

The development of larger four-barrel carburetors, far less finicky in practice than fuel-injection, helped spell the end for the Rochester fuelie setup in 1965. The debut of the 396 big-block also contributed to fuel injection's demise. Only 771 L84 F.I. Sting Rays were built for 1965.

LEFT
While a host of racing options had been available to Corvette buyers since 1957, Chevrolet really got the ball rolling in 1963, grouping all the hottest parts together in one package, labeled RPO Z06. Top fuelie power, heavy-duty suspension and special brakes were all included. Only 199 Z06 Sting Rays were built for 1963.

A performance powerplant from head to toe, the L78 396 pumped out 425 rompin', stompin' horses. Mandatory options included the close-ratio M20 Muncie four-speed, transistorized ignition (RPO K66) and a Positraction differential. Notice the optional power brakes with dual-circuit master cylinder.

LEFT
Much less costlier than the fuel injection, and considerably more powerful, was the 1965 396 Sting Ray, the first big-block Corvette. Price for the L78 big-block option was $292.70. Production of 396 Corvettes was 2,157.

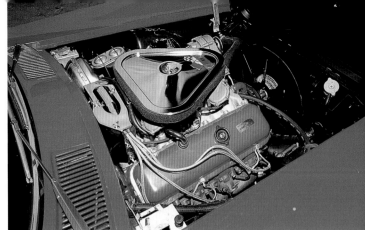

A distinctive triangular air cleaner was part of the L71 package. Under normal operation, the 435hp 427 was fed by the middle Holley two-barrel. Putting the pedal to the metal brought the other two carbs into play via a vacuum signal. When really wailing, the 3x2 setup sucked in some 1000cfm worth of fuel/air.

tank from the package to help whittle down RPO Z06's original $1,818.45 asking price. The 36.5-gallon tank, RPO N03, remained a separate option, able to be added to any Sting Ray coupe, Z06 or other model.

Reportedly, only 199 buyers chose a Z06 Sting Ray coupe in 1963. Amazingly, some of these customers bought these rough-and-ready rockets with intentions of driving them in everyday situations—not a smart move at all, considering the car's cantankerous demeanor. In the words of engineer/author Paul Van Valkenburgh, the Z06 Corvette "was not a car to drive on the street. It was noisy, rode hard, [and] the brakes were terrible—[they] wouldn't work at all until you warmed them up very, very well."

RPO Z06 made a brief repeat performance early in 1964, at least on paper. Ini-

LEFT
After big-block displacement was increased to 427ci in 1966, the Corvette's top performance V-8 was bumped up to 435hp in 1967, thanks to the addition of three Holley two-barrel carburetors. Listed under RPO L71, the tri-carb 427 found 3,754 buyers in 1967.

Meant only for off-road use, the L88 Sting Ray appeared in the spring of 1967 with nary a clue as to its ferocious demeanor. Price for the track-ready option was $947.90. Only 20 were built in 1967.

tially listed as a 1964 Sting Ray option, the Z06 package was quickly discontinued before any were sold. Chevrolet opted instead to offer the various Z06 components as separate options.

As brutish as the Z06 Sting Ray was, it was not the meanest Corvette built for 1963. That honor went to the Grand Sport, a purpose-built race car reminiscent of Duntov's ill-fated SS of 1957. Even though the 1957 AMA "ban" on factory racing supposedly closed the door on such shenanigans, Duntov never stopped thinking about building a world-class competition Corvette. And once performance-conscious Semon E. "Bunkie" Knudsen came over from Pontiac to be Chevrolet general manager in November 1961, Duntov was allowed just enough leeway to kick off another competition-minded project.

That project began in the summer of 1962, as Duntov's engineers began fashioning a special lightweight Corvette, based on a tubular-steel, ladder-type frame. Weight was also saved by using various aluminum components, Halibrand magnesium knock-off wheels, and a special handmade fiberglass body with super-thin panels. Some external dimensions were also changed to help improve on the stock Sting Ray's aerodynamics. Plexiglass windows, a 36.5-gallon fuel tank and enlarged wheelhouse openings for larger tires were incorporated. Brakes were large 11.75-inch Girling discs at all four corners.

Initial specifications called for a 377ci small-block fed by four Weber carbs for the Grand Sport. Early plans also mentioned a production run of 125 Grand Sports. Neither became reality. The first Grand Sport was fitted with an aluminum 327 fuelie while awaiting the 377 V-8 still in development. And before that work could be fin-

ished, GM announced a ban of its own, instructing all divisions in January 1963 to cease racing projects immediately.

Only the first five of the 125 planned Grand Sports escaped Chevrolet Engineering before that order came down. From there, each went through a steady progression of so-called independent race teams. They also underwent various mechanical and exterior modifications, taking on a varied succession of scoops, flares and engines. Both small-blocks and big-blocks were used over the years, and two of the coupes were later converted into roadsters for competition at Daytona in February 1964.

GM officials, however, stepped in again before those two roadsters could reach Florida. Clearly, Chevrolet Engineering was still supporting much of the Grand Sport racing effort, despite orders to the contrary a year before. This time GM executives instructed Knudsen to end these activities or risk his annual bonus. The five Grand Sports were then sold off. And the last major competition appearance came in 1966. Like the SS and SR-2s before them, all five Grand Sports survive today in collectors' hands.

Back on the street, the next great moment in Corvette history came in 1965, when four-wheel disc brakes were made standard equipment and two great powerplants crossed paths. Chevrolet's fuel-injected small-block—a major part of the Corvette mystique and the top power source since 1957—was offered for the last time in 1965. Its high $538 asking price was no longer justifiable, since less expensive, less finicky carbureted 327s had become nearly as powerful. Even more powerful was the all-new 396ci Mk IV V-8, the Corvette's first big-block.

Introduced early in 1965, the 396 featured

Beneath the 1967 L88's functional hood was the star of the show, the aluminum-head 427. The odd-looking air cleaner fit into special ductwork in the hood's underside from which it drew denser air from the base of the windshield. Also notice the black road draft tube running from the driver's side valve cover to behind the master cylinder. An L88 couldn't pass emissions tests since it simply vented its crankcase directly into the atmosphere.

a bullet-proof block and free-breathing cylinder heads with ball-stud rockers and large, canted valves. It was the perceived haphazard fashion in which these valves protruded upward that inspired the nickname "porcupine heads." These exceptional heads, in concert with a high-lift mechanical cam, 11:1 compression, transistorized ignition, a big

Holley four-barrel on an aluminum intake, and header-type cast-iron exhausts, helped the Mk IV big-block produce 425hp.

Mounting the 425hp 396 between fiberglass fenders required various modifications, the most noticeable being a bulging hood with functional louvers. Both chassis and driveline were beefed, cooling was improved, and a close-ratio four-speed and Positraction rearend were mandatory. What did all this heavy-duty equipment add up to? According to *Road & Track*, a 396 Corvette could turn the quarter-mile in 14.1 seconds, "quicker than any other standard production car we've tested except the AC Cobra."

But if the automotive press thought that was hot, they had another thing coming. The following year, the Mk IV was bored out to 427 cubic inches. Then in 1967, three Holley two-barrel carburetors were added atop the Corvette's 427, producing 435 real horsepower.

One of the best-working progressive throttle arrangements ever seen on an American multiple-carb setup, the optional "3x2" equipment was both efficient and hot to trot. Under normal driving, the middle two-barrel worked alone, pumping roughly 300cfm of fuel/air into the lazily loping L71 big-block. With the hammer dropped, a vacuum signal brought the other two carbs into action precisely, bringing total flow to about 1000cfm as all hell broke loose.

In *Car and Driver's* words, the 3x2 setup resulted "in an astoundingly tractable engine and uncannily smooth engine response." It also resulted in some serious neck injuries. *Cars* magazine's Martyn Schorr reported a best quarter-mile run of 12.9 seconds at 111mph for the L71 Corvette. Only five seconds were required to go from 0 to 60mph. Was it any wonder *Hot Rod's* Eric Dahlquist called the tri-carb Sting Ray the "hottest 'Vette yet?"

Actually, the hottest Corvette in 1967 was another racing-inspired Sting Ray, the legendary L88. Far more cantankerous than the 1963 Z06, the 1967 L88 Corvette was clearly not meant for the street, and Chevrolet wasn't afraid to admit this fact in the least. "Because

the L88 is an off-road engine," read a press release, "no provision has been made for anti-pollution control. For those states that require smog-control devices, it cannot be registered for street use in a passenger carrying vehicle." Another label found inside an L88 Sting Ray was even more foreboding. "Warning: Vehicle must operate on a fuel having a minimum of 103 research octane and 95 motor octane or engine damage may result."

While Chevrolet gave the L88 427 a token rating of "only" 430hp, actual output was probably upwards of 550 horses. Aluminum heads with large valves were part of the L88 deal, as were 12.5:1 pistons. And a huge 850cfm Holley four-barrel fed cooler, denser air by a specially ducted hood. Mandatory options included transistorized ignition, power-assisted metallic brakes, F41 sports suspension, Positraction and the indestructible M22 "Rocker Crusher" four-speed. Also included with the L88 package was RPO C48, the heater-defroster delete. Who needed such luxuries on a race track, right?

On the legendary track at Le Mans in France, one of the twenty L88 Corvettes built for 1967 impressed all with its dominating speed down the Mulsanne Straight. But a thrown rod halfway through the race ended yet another Corvette attempt at international racing glory. Not all was lost, however, as the aluminum-head L88 returned in 1968, and this time became a big SCCA winner while carrying the Owens-Corning Fiberglass banner. L88 production was 80 in 1968, followed by another 116 in 1969.

Although the second-generation Corvettes, the so-called "midyear" models of 1963-67, never produced the world-beater Duntov had hoped for, they didn't dim the original Sting Ray's reputation on the street in the least. They were great cars all.

BIG-BLOCKS BOW OUT

The life span for the second-generation Corvette, the mid-year models if you will, ran five years—one more than planned. Few, if any, fiberglass fans probably cared, however, especially when presented in 1967 with what many considered to be the best of the early Sting Ray breed. And to think the last of the mid-years basically represented a stop-gap of sorts.

Work on a re-styled, thoroughly modern second-edition Sting Ray had begun early in 1965, with high hopes of making that new ideal a production-line reality for 1967. But development problems delayed that debut, forcing Duntov, Mitchell and the rest to roll out one more mid-year model before the third generation finally bowed for 1968.

Inspired by stylist Larry Shinoda's Mako Shark II showcar of 1965, the 1968 Corvette

Originally listed at 370 hp in 1970, LT-1 performance dropped to 330 horses in 1971, then was net rated at 255 hp in 1972. Along with being a true road rocket, this 1972 LT-1 is also a movie star, having appeared in the 1995 hit, Apollo 13.

was quickly equated to a Coke bottle with its bulging front and rear quarters serving as bookends for a slimmed-down midsection. Comparing the new 1968 to its "pinched-waist" 1963-67 predecessor was akin to standing Raquel Welch up next to Lily Tomlin. Along with being some seven inches longer and considerably more shapely than its forerunner, the 1968 Corvette also scored higher in the sultry department. As *Car and Driver's* critics put it, "it's lusty, it stimulates all of the base emotion lurking deep in modern man. It is the *Barbarella* of the car maker's art"—an analogy in reference to the semi-psyche-delic, surely-sexploitive 1967 Dino De Laurentiis film starring Jane Fonda.

As for the stuff of legends, top power for the lusty 1968 Corvette once more came from the 427 big-block, again available in optional 435hp L71 3x2 form. The race-ready L88s were carryovers as well, for both 1968 and 1969. And those who wanted a piece of the L88 lightweight action, without all those off-

Chevrolet's third-generation Corvette received an all-new "Coke-bottle" body for 1968. Removable roof panels were also new that year. This 1968 coupe is powered by an aluminum-head L89 427. Priced at $805.75, the L89 option was checked off 624 times in 1968.

Originally introduced for the tri-carb L71 427 in 1967, the L89 aluminum-head option not only shaved off some unwanted pounds, it also added a revised combustion chamber and different valves. Advertised output, however, remained at 435hp. RPO L89 was discontinued after the last 427 was offered in 1969.

road limitations could add the L89 aluminum head option to their L71 427. First offered in 1967, the $832.05 L89 option attracted 624 buyers in 1968, after only 20 pairs were sold the previous year. Another 390 pairs went out the door in 1969. Although valves and combustion chambers differed slightly for the lightweight L89 heads compared to their cast-iron counterparts, no change in advertised output was made when they were added to the 435hp 427.

Even more aluminum was used in 1969, when Chevrolet unleashed two ZL-1 Sting Ray coupes, the last of the truly exotic Corvettes to make it to the streets. Featuring a pair of aluminum heads atop an aluminum cylinder block, the ZL-1 427 was not

for the timid—of spirit or wallet. Sticker price for RPO ZL-1 alone went well beyond four grand. Much more radical than the L88 throughout, the ZL-1 still carried the same token horsepower rating—430hp. Again, actual output soared past 500 horses, a fact quickly proven at the track where a 1969 ZL-1 Corvette wowed the press with a screaming 12.1-second quarter-mile pass. Trap speed was 116mph.

Plans for yet another high-powered aluminum-aided big-block for 1970 ran afoul of Chevrolet's latest "de-proliferation" plans. Originally listed in 1970 Corvette paperwork and tested by the press in prototype form, Chevy's stillborn LS-7 454ci big-block featured aluminum heads, 12.25:1 compres-

Identified by its nose stripe and bulging hood, this ZL1 Corvette is one of only two built for 1969, although others may have resulted from crated engines being delivered into private hands.

LEFT
Save for the air pump emission controls, the 1969 ZL1 427 looks very much like the L88. But unlike the L88, the ZL-1 has an aluminum cylinder block to accompany those aluminum heads. Chevrolet also used the all-aluminum ZL1 427 in Camaros for 1969.

RIGHT
The sexy, new 1968 Corvette measured seven inches longer than its 1967 forerunner and was nearly two inches shorter in height. Base big-block power came from a 390hp 427, as this Silverstone Silver coupe demonstrates.

Demonstrated here is the Corvette's biggest big-block, the 454ci Mk IV, which replaced the 427 in 1970. This 1971 LS5 454 Stingray is one of 5,097 built.

sion and 465hp—more than enough to put an LS-7 Sting Ray into the 13-second quarter-mile bracket, according to *Sports Car Graphic*. But growing corporate concerns over how much power was too much, led GM's front office to kill the LS-7 before it made regular production, leaving Corvette buyers to make do with the much more mundane 390hp LS-5 454.

Even with Detroit's horsepower race rounding its last turn, Chevy engineers did manage one last gasp in 1971 when they made the LS-6 454 a Corvette option. LS-6 features included open-chamber aluminum heads, a big dual-feed Holley four-barrel atop an aluminum intake, transistorized ignition, and a mechanical cam. Advertised output was 425hp. Quarter-mile performance was listed at 13.8 seconds by *Car and Driver*.

But big-block Corvettes weren't the only headline makers in the 1970s. Chevrolet's long-running small-block had been enlarged

again in 1969 to 350ci. And in 1970, the 350 was the base for the Corvette's hottest small-block since the 375hp L84 327 fuelie disappeared after 1965. Initially rated at five less horses than the L84, the LT-1 350 made for a better-balanced, more road-worthy Corvette, compared to the big, bullyish, nose-heavy Mk IV models. The LT-1 lineup included a solid-lifter cam, 11:1 compression, and a Holley four-barrel on an aluminum intake.

As for performance, a 1970 LT-1 ran right along with a Porsche 911 in a *Motor Trend* test. "Off the strip and onto the road course, this is where the Porsche should reign supreme," began *MT's* report. "Here is where

Captured at the National Corvette Museum, this 1971 LS6 Stingray is one of only 188 built. Behind it is an 1986 "Malcolm Konner Commemorative Edition" Corvette, one of 50 created by Malcolm Konner Chevrolet in Paramus, New Jersey.

we experienced the biggest surprise of the test. The [LT-1] Corvette was just as fast, if not faster, through the corners as the Porsche."

"It's a frustrated racer," claimed *Car and Driver*, "a fact it never lets you forget." After dropping to 330hp in 1971, the last of the first-generation LT-1s appeared in 1972 net rated at 255 horses.

For small-block fans who really wanted to give Porsche drivers a run for their money, Chevrolet also offered the ZR-1 package, an LT-1 Corvette with an M-22 four-speed, heavy-duty power brakes, special suspension and an aluminum radiator. Wearing a price tag of about $1000, RPO ZR-1 was offered each year along with the LT-1. Production was only 25 in 1970, eight in 1971 and 20 in 1972. A similar equipment group, RPO ZR-2, was made available along with the LS-6 big-block in 1971. Priced at $1,747, ZR-2 equipment found its way into a mere eight 425hp Sting Rays that year.

After 1971, much of the Corvette's serious sting fell by the wayside as Detroit's era of outlandish performance came to a close. Drastically lowered compression ratios in 1971 were followed by net-rated output figures the following year. Along with the 255hp LT-1, speed-conscious customers could also pick the 270hp 454 in 1972. But the Mk IV V-8 wasn't long for the world, either. Even though the Corvette's third-generation actually ran up through 1982, an end of an era came in 1974 when Chevrolet built its last big-block Corvette.

For Corvette buyers from then on, it was a small-block or no block at all.

Air conditioning typically wasn't available along with RPO LT-1 when the option debuted in 1970. Nor in 1971. But per Zora Duntov's orders, one 1972 LT-1 was taken off the line and tested with an air conditioning installation, resulting in the availability of air-conditioned LT-1 Corvettes by the end of the year. The 1972 LT-1 shown here is that very prototype.

RIGHT
Chevrolet's first-generation LT-1 Corvette was offered between 1970 and 1972 as a nimble small-block alternative to those big-block bullies. This 1972 LT-1 is one of 1,741 built.

CHEVROLET'S FIBERGLASS LEGACY LIVES ON

Let's face it, the late 1970s simply were bad years as far as Detroit performance was concerned. And America's only sports car was no exception. As if sky-high insurance costs and ever-growing safety concerns weren't enough to discourage the building of high-powered automobiles, tightening emissions standards were strangling the life out of the good ol' Yankee V-8. Once the doomed 454 big-block disappeared from the Corvette options list after 1974, drivers were left with a series of continually weakening 350 small-blocks.

But the situation started turning around by 1978, the year Chevrolet celebrated the Corvette's 25th birthday. Thanks to the optional 220hp L82 350, the 1978 Corvette was still king of the American hill, a fact not missed by *Car and Driver.* "We can happily report the 25th example of the Corvette is much improved across the board. Not only will it run faster now—the L82 version with four-speed is certainly the fastest American production car—but the general driveability and road manners are of a high order as well."

Along with that welcomed L82 shot in the arm, all 1978 Corvettes also received special 25th anniversary badges to mark the special occasion. And the 25th Corvette wore a new "fastback" rear window which both aided rearward vision and improved storage space behind the seats.

Additional commemoration was initially available through RPO B2Z, which added an exclusive two-tone silver anniversary paint scheme. Dual sport mirrors and aluminum wheels were required options, along with the paint. Production of these silver anniversary Corvettes was 15,283.

Another special 1978 model, the Limited Edition, marked that anniversary, as well as the Corvette's first appearance at Indianapolis

Chevrolet marked the first of three prestigious Indy Pace Car appearances for the Corvette with this Limited Edition model in 1978. Among a long list of features were the front air dam, aluminum wheels and rear spoiler. All 1978 Corvettes were 25th anniversary models.

It doesn't come much more distinctive than the optional silver leather interior on this 1978 Limited Edition Corvette. Not visible behind the steering wheel is an AM/FM 8-track stereo, included in the Limited Edition package.

as the prestigious pace car for the Indy 500. Priced at $13,653.21, compared to $9,351.89 for a base 1978 sport coupe, the Limited Edition Indy Pace Car replica was stuffed full of options. Included were power windows, door locks and antenna, removable glass roof panels, a rear window defogger, air conditioning, sport mirrors and a tilt-telescopic steering column. Other options included white-letter P225/60R15 tires, a heavy-duty battery, and an AM/FM 8-track stereo with dual rear speakers. A front air dam, a rear spoiler and aluminum wheels with red pinstripes completed the deal, which was originally intended to be of "limited" status, but ended up quite the contrary. When the feeding frenzy for what many felt would be a future

collectible came to a close, Chevrolet sold 6,502 of these high-profile fastbacks. Today, their collector value remains minimal.

Yet another special-edition model came four years later, just as the third-generation Corvette was bowing out. Like the 1978 silver anniversary Corvette, the 1982 Collector Edition featured unique paint, this time a silver-beige finish accented by graduated grey

RIGHT
As part of a charity fund-raising effort, the National Council of Corvette Clubs raffled off the very first of the all-new 1984 Corvettes, serial number 00001. In collector Dick Gonyer's hands today, the car is still identified on the doors and windshield as it was when originally raffled. This is the only #00001 model from any Corvette generation known to survive.

A Corvette convertible returned in 1986 just in time to become the second fiberglass two-seater from Chevrolet to pace the Indianapolis 500. This 1986 Indy Pace Car replica resides in the Klassix Auto Museum in Daytona Beach, Florida.

decals and pinstriping. Features included "hatchback" rear glass, special emblems, exclusive "turbine" alloy wheels wearing white-letter P255/60R15 rubber, a leather-wrapped steering wheel, matching silver-beige leather upholstery, and luxury carpeting. Removable glass roof panels done in unique bronze tinting, a rear window defogger, and a power antenna were also included in the package. The price for that package? Try about $22,500, up more than $4,000 beyond the base coupe's sticker. In chief engineer Dave McLellan's words, the

1982 Collector Edition was "a unique combination of color, equipment, and innovation to produce one of the most comprehensive packages ever offered to the Corvette buyer." Production was 6,759.

Window dressing aside, real history was made in March 1983 when Chevrolet finally introduced the all-new Corvette everyone had been waiting for— for nearly 15 years or roughly six months, depending on your perspective. The third-generation Corvette was a decade old when Dave McLellan began envisioning a redesigned next generation early in 1978. Initially it appeared his vision would become reality in 1983, but various stumbling blocks delayed that debut, which would have been

E ven past 40,
America's sports car keeps rolling along in impressive fashion. ■

in the fall of 1982. While 43 pre-production third-generation 1983 Corvettes were built, none were released to the public, and only one still survives today. Chevrolet skipped over the 1983 model and introduced its next generation Corvette as a 1984 with an extended production run.

Everything about the car was new, from its modern chassis, to its roomier interior, and its re-styled body. Created by GM designer Jerry Palmer, the 1984 Corvette shell was state-of-the-art in both form and function. Its drag coefficient was .34, down nearly 25 percent in comparison to the body left behind in 1982. Beneath that shell was an innovative "bird cage" structure integrated with a "backbone-type" frame that mounted the drivetrain from engine to

LEFT
They called it the King of the Hill, and for good reason. Chevrolet's first ZR-1 was easily the most dominating street-going Corvette ever built. With a superb suspension, loads of rubber and 375 horses beneath its clamshell hood, the 1990 ZR-1 could run with anything in this country, and almost anything worldwide.

Like its forefather 35 years previously, all 1988 35th anniversary Corvettes were white. This external identification was included in the $4,795 package listed under RPO Z01.

Four cams, 32 valves and all-aluminum construction certainly qualified the ZR-1's LT5 V-8 as the most exotic production Corvette powerplant ever. Rated at 375hp from 1990 to 1992, the LT5 was pumped up to 405 horses for 1993-95.

The 40th anniversary Corvette's Ruby Red color scheme carried over into the interior. Headrests also included special "40th" logo embroidery.

differential as one rigid component joined by an aluminum C-section beam. Suspension was totally new, with fiberglass transverse monoleaf springs in the front and rear. Aluminum and other lightweight materials were used wherever possible to cut unwanted pounds.

Sixteen-inch cast-aluminum wheels measured a half inch wider in back. The four-wheel disc brakes had semi-metallic linings and aluminum calipers. The engine was a 205hp L83 Cross Fire 5.7-liter V-8. A choice was offered between a four-speed automatic or 4+3 Doug Nash manual (with overdrives in the top three gears). All this and more came standard with the 1984 Corvette. More than 51,000 were sold during the extended production run, kicking off the third generation in grand fashion.

Two years later, a convertible returned to the Corvette lineup after a nine-year hiatus. And it appeared just in time to pace the 70th running of the Indy 500 on May 25, 1986. For the second time, a collection of high-profile Corvette Indy Pace Car replicas was marketed to the public. A third Corvette would pace the lead lap at Indianapolis in 1995, spawning yet another group of Pace Car replicas.

Late in 1986, the first in a series of truly tough Corvettes appeared on the lot of a New Jersey Chevrolet dealership founded by Malcolm Konner. Konner Chevrolet put together 50 of its "Malcolm Konner Commemorative Edition" Corvettes, one of which was then retrofitted with a twin-tur-

Yet another birthday present to Corvette customers arrived in 1993, and exclusive paint was once more part of the package.

bocharged engine supplied by Callaway Cars, Inc., now of Old Lyme, Connecticut. Reeves Callaway, Callaway Cars founder, had been toying since 1977 with aftermarket turbo modifications of various models, from BMW to Volkswagen. But the Konner installation was just a stepping stone towards Callaway's biggest break—an agreement with Chevrolet to build the Callaway Twin Turbo Corvette.

Chevrolet officially assigned the Callaway package an RPO code, B2K, in June 1986. Production began the following month and the Twin Turbo killer Corvette debuted as a 1987 model. Chevrolet shipped fully assembled 1987 Corvettes to Callaway Cars where they were converted into Twin Turbos. Although the price for the "option" alone was $19,995, those in the need for speed couldn't have cared less. With 345hp, a 1987 Callaway Corvette could reportedly hit 177mph. One-hundred-eighty-four were built that first year. RPO B2K stayed on the Corvette options list through 1991.

With 345hp, a 1987 Callaway Corvette could reportedly hit 177mph. ∎

Meanwhile, back in the regular-production world, Chevrolet again marked a fiberglass birthday in 1988 with a special 35th anniversary Corvette. Like the first Corvette in 1953, the 35th anniversary model came only in white. White leather sport buckets with anniversary headrest embroidery and a commemorative console plaque were also part of the deal. Power seats, air conditioning, a sport handling package, and external identification were included as well. Price for the package was $4,975; 2,050 were built.

The legendary "King of the Hill," the ZR-1, debuted as a 1990 model after the public was teased with a prototype introduction in 1989. The heart of this beast was the 375hp LT5 5.7-liter V-8, engineered by Lotus in

Callaway Cars' Twin Turbo Speedster of 1991 surely looked every bit as outrageously as it ran. Designed by Paul Deutschman, the Speedster's shell was best recognized for its cutdown windscreen and eye-popping paint schemes done in purple, yellow, green, orange or blue. Beneath those twin scoops was a 450hp 5.7-liter small-block fed by twin, intercooled turbochargers. Price for this beast was about $150,000.

Rarest of the 1993 40th anniversary Corvettes was the ZR-1 coupe. Only 245 were built. Even more special is this particular 40th anniversary ZR-1, which was modified by aftermarket builder Doug Rippie Motorsports. Only eight ZR-1s received DRM's emissions-legal "Black Widow" touch.

England and built by Mercury Marine in Stillwater, Oklahoma. Dual overhead cams, four valves per cylinder and an all-aluminum construction were just the beginning of the LT5's innovative appeal.

As for the rest of the package, ZR-1 brakes were huge—13 inches in front, 12 in the rear. And in order to house the equally huge Goodyear Eagle 315/35ZR-17 GS-C tires required in back to handle all that power, the ZR-1 received an exclusive widened tail section with unique square taillights. ABS and Z51 suspension were also included.

Whether in the curves or flat-out, the ZR-1 was a world-class street killer. Its time-honored 0-60 clocking was only 4.9 seconds. Quarter-mile performance came in at 13.4 seconds with a 108mph trap speed.

The DRM Black Widow LT5 got its name from its black finish. Thanks to, among other things, different cams and precise head work, the DRM LT5 produced 475hp. Also part of the Doug Rippie conversion was coilover shock front suspension.

Chevrolet introduced this eye-catching Copper Metallic finish for the Corvette in 1994, only to find it quite difficult to apply evenly. Because of this, the shade was discontinued early in the run. Reportedly, only 110 1994 Copper Metallic Corvettes were released, 86 coupes and 24 convertibles.

Superior sports car appeal carried over in typically stunning fashion for 1995. Improvements included better ride quality and the addition of larger (13-inch rotors in place of the 12-inch units used in 1994) heavy-duty standard brakes.

Top end was nearly 180mph. All this dominating power did, however, come at a price. ZR-1 equipment added around $25,000 to the $32,000 normal asking price for a 1990 Corvette coupe. While that figure didn't deter diehards at first, it did help limit the car's appeal. Actual production never did reach projections, not even after Chevrolet leapfrogged the 1993 ZR-1 over the Viper as the most powerful car in America by upping the LT5 ante to a whopping 405hp.

After 3,049 ZR-1 Corvettes were built the first year, production rapidly declined as the gleam wore off; even more so after Chevrolet introduced its second-generation LT1 in 1992. ZR-1 production dropped to 2,044 for 1991, 502 for 1992, and 448 for 1993, 1994 and 1995. According to Chevrolet general manager Jim Perkins, both the success of the much less expensive LT1 Corvette and the rising costs associated with continuing the ZR-1's limited production run helped spell the end for the King of the Hill.

After taking away a bit of the ZR-1's exclusive outward appeal by adding the

he legendary "King of the Hill," the ZR-1, debuted as a 1990 model after the public was teased with a prototype introduction in 1989. ∎

widened tail to all Corvettes in 1991, Chevrolet really knocked the knees out from under the King of the Hill in 1992. New that year was a truly hot pushrod small-block, the second-generation LT1. Producing 300hp, the latest in Chevy's long line of 5.7-liter small-blocks went a long way toward tempting Corvette buyers to save their $25-30,000 and stick with standard Corvette performance. A 1992 LT1 could hit 60mph in 5.7 seconds, while the quarter-mile went by 8.4 ticks later. Top end was listed at a tad more than 160mph. LT1 muscle was just what the doctor ordered to revive the Corvette's spirits going into its fourth decade on the road.

To mark that special anniversary, Chevrolet once again rolled out a birthday edition. Wearing a price tag of $1,455, RPO Z25—Chevrolet's 40th anniversary appearance package—was available on all 1993 Corvettes, LT1

On August 28, 1995, the last of Chevrolet's 6,938 ZR-1 Corvettes rolled off the Bowling Green assembly line before an assembled crowd of company officials and press, signaling the end of the six-year run for the King of the Hill.

91

In its final form, the revered LT5 V-8 still pumped out 405hp, as it had since 1993. Adding those 30 additional horses was basically a matter of maximizing what already existed. Engineers simply ported and polished the cylinder heads.

coupes and convertibles, as well as the brawny ZR-1. Thrown in as part of the deal was exclusive Ruby Red metallic paint with matching leather inside, color-keyed wheel centers, 40th anniversary logos, and chromed emblems for the hood and fuel filler door. Additional special identification also appeared on the Ruby Red leather bucket seats in the form of "40th" logo headrest embroidery. Production for the Z25 1993 Corvette was 4,333 coupes, 2,171 convertibles and 245 ZR-1s.

Even past forty, America's sports car keeps rolling along in impressive fashion. Improvements to the LT1's induction gear helped the 1994 Corvette feel even stronger than the 1993, even though advertised output remained at 300hp. Minor overall improvements have followed, but how

LEFT
As in 1982, Chevrolet has put together a special Collector Edition model to honor an outgoing generation before the next new one arrives. The exclusive paint and interior treatment are part of the deal, as is the new 330hp LT4 V-8 if the buyer so chooses.

LEFT
The new LT4 small-block is standard for the 1996 Grand Sport, optional on all other Corvettes. Its 30 additional horses, compared to the standard 300hp LT1, will be warmly welcomed.

RIGHT
Painted to revive memories of its racing name-sakes from earlier days, the 1996 Grand Sport is offered in coupe and convertible form. Plans call for about 1000 to be built, all identical externally.

much more can Chevrolet improve on what ranks as one of the world's best performance machines at the price? Just take a look.

New for 1996 is an optional 5.7-liter V-8, the LT4. Like its still-strong LT1 cousin, the LT4 has aluminum heads, roller lifters and sequential-port fuel injection. But various improvements, including a more aggressive cam, better breathing heads, upgraded, higher-flowing injection, and 10.8:1 compression (up from the LT1's 10.4:1), help bump output up from 300 horses to 330hp. Although it is available for all 1996 Corvettes, the LT4 is the standard powerplant for the Grand Sport special-edition models. Only the six-speed manual comes behind the LT4

Inspired by Duntov's five lightweight Grand Sport racers of 1963, the new Grand Sport features an exclusive competition-type paint scheme. All of the approximately 1000 Grand Sport coupes and convertibles planned for 1996 will be painted Admiral

Blue Metallic with white racing stripes and red "Sebring-style" hash marks on the driver's side front fender. Various bits of special identification, 17-inch black aluminum wheels, black brake calipers with bright "Corvette" lettering, and special bucket seats are part of the Z16 package. Grand Sport coupes receive P275/40ZR-17 rubber up front and P315/35ZR-17 in the rear, with a pair of fender flares added in back to help house the wider tires. Grand Sport convertible tires are P255/45ZR-17 (front) and P285/40ZR-17 (back).

A second special-edition Corvette for 1996 also follows in another earlier model's tracks. Like its 1982 counterpart, the 1996 Collector Edition has arrived to salute the last of the latest generation of Corvettes before the next all-new model arrives. Exclusive Sebring Silver paint, special identification, silver 17-inch aluminum wheels, black brake calipers with bright "Corvette" lettering, and "Collector Edition" embroidery inside make up what Chevrolet calls an "eminently collectible" offering. As with base models, the LT1 is standard for the 1996 Collector Edition, with the LT4 available at extra cost.

Whether or not this newest Collector Edition Corvette will end up being eminently collectible is anyone's guess. Ask again a few more generations down the road.

INDEX